Listen Up!

For Roo's Tea Room

Best Wishes

Christina Gabbitas :)

#staysafe

Compiled by Christina Gabbitas
All the poems in this book are the work of the authors, and no words have been changed in the process of compiling this book. Some words have been replaced by an asterisk.
Authors: Children and young people
Illustrator: Alicia Abbott
Copyright: Christina Gabbitas Writing Ltd

Any proceeds from book sales will be donated to NSPCC Childline: 216401 and SCO37717

Listen Up!

poems & lyrics by young people about county lines exploitation and knife crime

About the book

Author and Honorary Member of the NSPCC Council, Christina Gabbitas, has been collaborating with various police forces and organisations since 2019 to educate children and young people about the intricate issues surrounding county lines exploitation and knife crime, through her engaging stories. She firmly believes in the power of storytelling as a means to effectively convey these important messages to her audience.

Having delivered sessions in both primary and secondary schools, Christina has witnessed first-hand the gaps in knowledge about exploitation. After hearing many heartbreaking stories and engaging with individuals who have lived through these experiences, she recognised that not all young people feel they have a choice in these matters. This realisation fuelled her desire to encourage greater collaboration among forces and organisations on a national level.

This initiative was inspired by a pupil from Rossett High in Harrogate, who independently submitted a poem following a session with Christina and North Yorkshire Police. Christina invited young people aged 12-21 to write a poem or song that reflects the realities of county lines exploitation and associated knife crime.

The poems and lyrics in this publication have enabled children and young people to have their voices heard.

For more details about the competition, please visit (http://www.trappedincountylines.co.uk/competition).

Special thanks to North Yorkshire Police, who have part funded this project with money seized from criminals, as well as YMCA Lincolnshire, Dean Coady OBE of Pure Urban Solutions, and Christina Gabbitas, who all helped with funding.

Contents

The Shadows of Destiny - Alexandru Cocosila 1

Listen Up! Beba Stokes... 3

Him – Grace Lakey 5

The Flower on her Deathbed – Angel Botfield................................ 9

Blades of Silence – Imogen Johnston... 11

Illusory – Kemaree.. 13

Exploitation - Brayden Hartley.. 15

The Day Everything Changed – Cieran Holt-Wolstenholme............ 16

Life Story – Ethan J.. 17

The Drug Cycle – Eleanor Burkert.. 19

No Turning Back - Amelia Godward.. 20

Equals - Emily Green... 21

Knife Crime - Keegan Want... 22

Shadow of the Lines - Daniel Johnson-Kenny.............................. 23

Missing – Alexander James Barker... 24

Deep Thoughts – Zak KP... 25

In Too Deep – Lamees Abdullah... 27

You Lied – Hally Yates.. 28

Losing Control – James McKenzie... 29

You Lied – Lola Pryce... 30

County Lines – Lily Tyrer.. 31

Whispers of the Trade - Imogen Johnston..................................... 33

Trapped – Hansen Gunby... 35

County Lines Uncool – Kenzo Kanapka... 37

The Knife Angel – Amelia Houghton.. 39

Mama - Zara Khanam... 41

Dark Clouds – Unaisah Dawud... 43

Strange Guy - Lena Rojan... 45

Gangs will be Gone - William Hickton... 47

Shattered Blades - Ruby Jones.. 49

Trapped - Immy Dunn and Sofia Pollack... 51

Trapped 2 -Immy Dunn and Sofia Pollack... 52

A Last Resort - Emma Jump.. 53

Part 1 - "I am scared" - Ibrahim Dawud.. 55

Part 2 - "The Long Despair" - Ibrahim Dawud.................................... 56

Time - Summer Bartlet... 57

It's Never Just One Time - Ffyon Burnham.. 58

My Story - Keziah Needham.. 59

That Life - Steve Croshaw... 60

Knife Sentence - Quinton Milisé... 61

Invisible Kid - Dean Coady... 63

Alone - Christina Gabbitas.. 64

Trapped in County Lines - Christina Gabbitas, Adam Baybutt and Millthorpe School Pupils, York... 65

Winner - The Shadows of Destiny

Alexandru Cocosila, 15

In a world of shadows deep,
Where young souls in turmoil weep,
Forced by fate's unkind decree
To sell their dreams for currency.

Their laughter lost, their innocence stolen,
In the darkness, their hopes lie broken.
Trapped in a cycle of despair,
Their hearts burdened with a heavy wear.

Each day a struggle to survive,
Their dreams fading, barely alive.
Caught in a web of lies and deceit,
Their spirits crushed beneath defeat.

But within each troubled heart's dark night,
A flicker of hope still burns bright,
Yearning for a way to break free,
To reclaim their lost dignity.

So let us reach out with a helping hand
To lift them up and help them stand,
To guide them towards a brighter way
And lead them to a brighter day.

2nd - Listen Up!

Beba Stokes, 14

Yo, listen up, let me tell you a tale
'Bout County Lines, it ain't no fairytale.
It's a serious biz, but we'll keep it light,
So grab a seat and let's take flight.

From the city to the countryside,
Where the hustle's on, no place to hide,
They're moving stuff, but it ain't right
Pushing drugs, causing a fight.

County Lines, it's a game they play,
But we gotta educate, that's the only way.
So, here's the deal, let's spread the news,
Stay away from trouble, don't follow their clues.

They recruit the young, it's a sad affair,
Promises of cash, but it leads to despair.
Phones buzzing, messages non-stop,
But trust me, kid, you gotta make it stop.

They'll use you up, then throw you away.
In this dangerous game, there's no time to play.
But hey, don't fret, there's hope in sight:
Stay true to yourself, keep up the fight.

County Lines, it's a game they play,
But we gotta educate, that's the only way.
So, here's the deal, let's spread the news,
Stay away from trouble, don't follow their clues.

Take a stand, don't be a pawn.
Together we can break the chain, and it's gone.
Spread love, not drugs, that's the key.
Let's build a better world, you and me.

County Lines, it's a game they play,
But we gotta educate, that's the only way.
So, here's the deal, let's spread the news,
Stay away from trouble, don't follow their clues.

Yeah, that's right, County Lines ain't cool.
Let's be smart and not be fooled.
Educate, communicate, let's make a change,
And, together, we'll rearrange.

3rd Place - Him

Grace Lakey ,13

He approached us in the middle of March.
Taylor, Sophia, and Connor were scared.
He told us he was a friend, he really, really cared.
I was crying and he noticed.
My parents never understand what they are doing to me,
Arguing about this and that.
In school, it is so hard to focus,
Swarming my mind like locusts.
He asked me for my phone number,
I didn't think twice.
Talking every day, giving me advice.
I could talk about my family and how they never noticed,
Reassuring me when I was at my lowest.
Taylor was the first to say I had changed,
I was becoming more estranged.
She said that I never talked to her anymore,
I was ignoring her, which had never happened before.
Sophia agreed and said I was always texting.
I didn't agree with what they were suggesting.
One day, he asked to meet up with me,
But my friends had booked a new movie to see.
I blew my friends off, he needed me more.
He met me in the street, just outside a store.
He handed me the newest trainers, just my size!
They were so expensive, I couldn't believe my eyes!
He looked at me wide-eyed,
Then handed me a parcel, a brown paper bag.
He told me to not look inside,
That it wasn't part of the plan.
I was puzzled, but he was my friend.
All I had to do was keep it where it would blend.
I agreed and put it in my pocket.
When I got home, he said I was part of the street gang,
That I had really proved myself, just as my phone rang.

He called and said he would introduce me to his friends,
If my job works out, it all just depends.
I put the paper bag under my mattress.
Part of me still wondered if I should look,
But I didn't want to lose my new-found happiness.
We continued to talk and he was so nice.
He made me feel special, but it came with a price:
Not having my friends.
That week he bought me the latest phone.
I couldn't believe it, it must have cost thousands!
He said I was the prettiest girl he had ever met,
That a nice girl like me should not have to go into debt.
No one had ever told me something like that.
He said he would go out with me,
If this time I did a bigger job for him, it wouldn't be free.
He picked me up that same day,
But this time at midnight.
He texted,
"Get the little brown bag and stay out of sight."
I was curious, but didn't ask questions.
I left a note for mum in case she got worried,
But, knowing her, she would never notice.
We drove for hours.
We were heading out of the city and into the next.
We arrived at an old house.
It was covered in dirt and grime.
Walking up felt more like a climb.
He had given me a drink on the way.
I handed over the paper bag as I started to sway.
Him and his friends just looked like a blur,
Spinning, spinning, spinning.
Hot, tingling breath was heavy on my neck,
Whispering, " I will be back."
In the morning, everyone was gone,
The door locked.
He was coming back for me, but I was stuck.
I knew he wouldn't hurt me, he cared about me.

I was left for four days,
Zero contact.
I started to worry and called him so many times.
He said I was ruining the plan,
This is not what girlfriends do.
The police found me, eventually.
They explained I had been used,
That I was part of a county line.
I was scared back then.
But I know the truth,
I should never have talked to him.
He hurt me, he never cared.
It was all
Him.

JULIA

The Flower on her Deathbed

Angel Botfield, 15

I don't know her favourite colour
Or the clothes she used to wear,
But I know where she is now,
And I know most people don't care.

I think she was a charming girl,
Not a lot of people knew.
I think she had a hard life,
A life she soon outgrew.

No one could tell what was going on
Or where she would go at night.
Her mother called the police often,
But the girl put up a fight.

She changed her favourite colour,
She changed the clothes she wore.
She ended up drowned in grey,
With a mattress on the floor.

Her time in custody was short-lived,
As she got let out just fine.
But that just made her life worse,
As her mental health was to decline.

She started getting more jobs
From the highest people in the scheme.
Until finally, someone wasn't happy
And her life ended in a scream.

Now I'm above her headstone,
With other flowers enveloping me,
Hearing stories of her life.
At least now, she is free.

I know she's in the ground,
Lying in a grave.
I know she will never water me
And I know, to society,
She will no longer be a slave.

ALICIA

Blades of Silence

Imogen Johnston, 14

Amidst the city's heartbeat,
Blades of silence carve tales untold,
Whispers of steel in shadows,
Where stories of sorrow and resilience unfold.

In the quietness of midnight,
Where darkness and despair entwine,
Echoes of footsteps linger,
As blades of silence continue to define.

In the tapestry of shadows,
Where secrets dance in moonlit rhyme,
A city's heartbeat falters,
Haunted by the spectre of a silent crime.

Beneath the shroud of starlit alleys,
A clandestine waltz unfolds.
Blades whisper tales of choices,
In the dance of destinies, stories untold.

Each silent step, a heartbeat's echo,
A symphony of shadows plays.
Yet within the silence, a plea emerges,
For a city's soul redemption sways.

As blades weave
Tales of tragic choices,
The city sighs,
Burdened by the weight.

In each silent blade,
A collective echo,
Lives disrupted,
Dreams dissipate.

A stain on the tapestry of unity,
Knife crime's venom spreads wide,
Tears etched in the city's heartbeat,
A collective plea, a call to cast aside.

Illusory

Kemaree, 15

Got tired of seeing no food in the fridge.
I hit the trap just to see how it is.
Mummy don't want me in this life that I live,
But the money come quick at 14, couple bills seem legit.
I didn't know who to trust, seen bare guys who I put in work for take more than the mick.
Really and truly, it is what it is.
Tryna do this music, so I can get a hit.
Mum said the badness don't pay, but the shots that I made had me feel kind of rich.

Didn't care about no one's feeling but mine.
I weren't stingy, I never left broski behind,
Really put my life on the line.
I'm not tryna be a risk and start letting of carbine,
But if anyone touches my bread and tries leave me with crumbs, then I'm losing my mind.
I watched this story plenty of times.
I know guys died, but cool, I'm alive.

The gwop came and went.
All the times I did legs for some freedom, it didn't make sense,
And everyone knows I got sense.
But I still waste my life for a 3.5 and a likkle benz.
Would have thought that I learned, but my mind went left,
Swinging these shanks and hope they don't bend.

Tryna make a rack, now I need like ten.
If not, then it's back to the trap house again.
Really this whole thing's mental: pray I don't get taken on the streets,
'cause I lost a couple friends.
Wishing I was still with them, but there ain't no rules when you mess with death.
Didn't even know if the product was mine - build up a zoot and mixing greens with blem.
Hope it's something that's gonna take my head.
I feel stress, hope I'm blessed,
pissed off and it got me vexed.
Trapped in a cycle, it feels like a hex.
Could've died there, that was the opp boys ends.
Likkle boy skipping school, hit the blocks till I heard that pops got locked.
More time, I wondered, maybe jail was the spot.
The line would still bang, if one of them drop.

No Franklin, but I'm always going to stay with my chop,
Because I can't get taken out by a single opp.
I remember times in school, thinking I was gonna get done,
Cuz I knew they were lurking, on these streets,
 I won't lie it wasn't worth it.
I lost my heart and I do need a surgeon.
I caused pain and countless of hurting.
But money needs to come and, Mum, I'm that person.

Exploitation

Brayden Hartley, 18

Exploitation and manipulation.
Something that started with just one conversation.
Showered in gifts, false promises too.
The vulnerable kids, who can't see through.
Glorifying gangs, not knowing the danger.
A so-called friend, but in truth it's a stranger.

Recruiting the youth, using innocence as a key,
Unlocking doors to a dark reality.
Snapchat and Instagram, we're too comfortable on these apps,
Giving up info, walking into traps.
A constant task, a scary situation,
Something that started with just one conversation.

Each drop-off worse, becoming more intense.
Carrying our own knives, as a self-defence,
No intent to use it, but others will.
These dangerous holders with an intent to kill.
One unhappy thug leading them to frustration.
Your life could be gone, starting with one conversation.

The Day Everything Changed

Cieran Holt-Wolstenholme, 17

The day everything changed,
I got pushed over the edge.
I trusted a person who got in my head.
They bought me nice things:
Trainers and clothes.

The day everything changed,
They lured me,
Told me to transport everything their way.
Train or by bus, they did not care,
As long as it got there with time to spare.

The day everything changed,
They would threaten me.
I was exactly what they wanted me to be.
It was money for them and violence for me.
I wanted to find a way out
Of the vicious cycle they kept quiet about.

The day everything changed.
I now receive support.
I have been saved from what I was taught.
I hope someday they will be caught,
To put rest to my distraught.
The day everything changed.

Life Story

Ethan J, 19

In my life, I have no clue what to do,
Just playing peekaboo with Scooby Doo,
Looking at the shit you always do.
Don't give a f***, I always come thru'.

Got in the game with no luck,
Still had my rambo tucked.
Police, I couldn't give two f****.
Sat in the station, I huffed and puffed.

When I got caught with sweets,
Got given remand for that.
My man broke the code
Whilst I sat there freezing cold.

Now, he's thinking, when's he free,
When's he making it home?
But I knew he broke
As soon as he phoned my phone.

When I got stabbed on the lack,
I reached for my strap
And it weren't there on my back.
Now, I'm out with a pack,
Trying to piece a glock with a mag.

Everyday, OT in a stolen ride
Tryna get by, not tryna die,
Only tryna survive.

Everyday, I'm getting high,
Look straight up to the blue, blue sky.
Little man, me nan, and me grandad,
Say my final goodbyes, 'cause I weren't there on the day that you died.

You wanna know why
Shit going on through my mind,
And now I'm walking around blind,
And everyday I'm getting fined.

Walking round OT, getting pulled
By bizzies who got schooled.
Now, they're jumping in their car,
Looking like fools.

I used to go pub just to play pool.
Nowadays, am getting made to look like a tool,
'Cause this shit that we do ain't cool.
But have to make a living somehow,
Just so we are able to eat our food.

The Drug Cycle

Eleanor Burkert, 14

It started with a vape,
Then some more,
Till you can't escape
And you're down on the floor.
Alone.

With no home,
You're stuck in the cycle of drugs.
When your delivery went wrong,
Life's not a song.
The drugs in your veins
Begin to take place.
You're left in this hell,
With no one to tell,
Lost in the cycle of drugs.

No Turning Back

Amelia Godward, 14

Problems hit the boy like bricks:
Not enough mates,
Dying to get the latest clothes or gadgets,
No money,
No food.
Dark house,
Boarded up windows, and smashed glass.
At the park, two boys wait for him.
One hands him a bag.
Just one try.
But then once turns to twice,
And twice turns to every day.
He skips school for the day, thinking this is fine,
He won't get anywhere in school anyway.
But again, one day turns to the week.
His teachers call home, but no answer.
Socials at the door, banging at two in the morning.
No escape.
No turning back.

Equals

Emily Green, 13

A phone, one you didn't ask for,
Equals a debt.
A debt, one you didn't ask for,
Equals money.
Money, the only thing you asked for,
Equals another debt.
A cycle, one you didn't ask for,
Equals hell.

Knife Crime

Keegan Want, 13

Those that say words cut like a knife,
Have the privilege of a life without strife.
Where walking the street can get you grief,
Man got beef,
Just for being me.

Blades of steel,
The fear is real.
Now, my face is about to peel.
What will it reveal?

Because knife crime, knife crime, be put in jail for a lifetime.

Jail, jail, begging for bail.
Mandem locked up.
None of them you can see,
Wanting to be free.
Now, we just let them be.

Lifetime, lifetime, shortened by knife crime.

Shadow of the Lines

Daniel Johnson-Kenny, age 14

In the shadow of the night, county lines
Blur wrong and right.
I thought it would be one simple favour.
Now, I'm stuck; I need a life-saver.
Drowned and desolate in this situation,
Dealing these drugs will be my suffocation.
Please, I just want to go home, but all I have is
This burner phone.

Missing

Alexander James Barker, 13

As I ponder through the deprived streets,
Heading to my friend's house, I feel off.
Arrived. I hear something I never thought would happen.
Something tells me it'll end badly.
I'm selected to deliver vapes and drugs. 'Sound,' I accepted.
My first delivery, it felt as if I was being watched.
Quickly, a man snatched my bag and stole the drugs: I now owe £300.
'I can't go back,' I thought, as it was too much.
I hesitate, but I go with it,
Never to be seen again.

Deep Thoughts

Zak KP, 18

They say they've been thru' it,
But they ain't ever been homeless.
They ain't got no backbone,
Them boys, der boneless.
I grew up with drinkers and grew up with stoners,
Then we grew up with bikes and motors,
Smoking on big buds, giving off odours.
As a YG, never listened to the olders.
One man army, I don't need no soldiers,
A'l fight thru' the pain, feel it on my shoulders.

I think it hurt the most when my dad passed.
Eight yrs ago, how's the time gone fast?
Rewind the clocks, let me rewind back,
'Cause there's so many questions I wanna ask.
I went off the rails, now I'm known in a mask.
I'm known to plod and all of that.
Started smashin' shit up when I get mad.
Think it's safe to say, av had a rocky past.

But atm, lemme f*** up this track,
Lemme f*** it up with this real rap.
This generation just rap for cash,
I rap on beats to please my dad.
I rap abar my life, not blades and macs.
'Cus Alf, u boys don't carry straps.
Yers js flex on socials, on different apps,
Addin' different captions, tryna act all mad.

I'm a quiet kid, keep myself to myself.
If I have problems, put 'em on a shelf.
All this shit's f***** my mental health
And recently A'v not been myself x2.

If I feel low, I js blaze up weed.
Think I'm addicted to these Cali trees
And I love them big nugs comin' green.
I'm havin' dreams that my music's seen.
I'm the new kid on the music scene,
Will I take over? Only time will see.
Until then, I'm gonna stack my p
And I want to be known on every street.

In Too Deep

Lamees Abdullah, 14

In too deep,
You make me out to be a sheep.
I took the leap,
Now, you've made me weep.
I feel like I can't say 'no',
Because you won't let me go.
I stored drugs in my car.
You sent me too far.
All I want to do is sleep.
I'm in too deep.

You Lied

Hally Yates, 14

You lied,
Then I cried,
I almost died.
It seemed like a good deal.
Now, I don't know how to feel.
You take things too far,
You even tried to steal my car.
All alone,
With only my burner phone.

Losing Control

James McKenzie, 13

It started innocent, everything in control,
But the more and more I did,
The more I lost control.
It started out nice,
Offers and offers,
Deals and deals,
I gain money, but I lose control.
Now, I am getting blackmailed,
Getting more lost in debt,
Losing safety, losing control,
Taking things too far.
Change from innocent to illegal.
Forced to do deeds,
Forced to lose control.

You Lied

Lola Pryce, 13

I thought I was sane,
You made it so real.
When I realized you led,
My hands were tied.
Being so trusting
Was never too good.
And when I knew
You lied,
I knew this was no good.

County Lines

Lily Tyrer, 14

Crossing county lines,
A dangerous game
In the shadows of the night,
Chasing fortune and fame,
Lost in the haze of a risky venture,
Leaving behind safety for a dangerous adventure.
County lines,
A path unknown,
Where danger lurks,
Seeds are sown.
Crossing border, a risky dance
in search of luck, taking a chance.

Whispers of the Trade

Imogen Johnston, 14

Whispers of the trade
Amidst the city's restless veins.
Where shadows stretch and secrets lie,
A network weaves through silent lanes,
County lines where whispers fly.

In the heart of night, the trade unfolds,
Young lives ensnared by empty dreams.
Through whispered calls and silent codes,
They chase a life that's not what it seems.

In the quiet still of hidden tracks,
Desperation fuels the chase.
Innocence lost, no turning back,
A fleeting glimpse of a familiar face.

Each journey taken, a silent scream,
Of choices made, of paths misled.
Through darkened streets where shadows teem,
With every step, a future bled.

Amid the towns and countryside,
Where hope and fear are thinly veiled,
The silent march of those who hide
In a game where countless have failed.

In every line, a silent cry,
For lost childhoods and broken homes.
A plea for help that won't deny
The chance to break from undertones.

As county lines weave dark designs,
The city sighs, the burden grows.
With every trade, the pain aligns,
Innocence fades as the network sows.

But in the midst of silent cries,
A call for justice, loud and clear,
To sever bonds, to break the ties,
And end the cycle built on fear.

Trapped

Hansen Gunby, 19

I should've stayed in school.
I realise now it is too late.
The second I joined this group,
The sweet taste of money led to my fate.

My mother always told me to stay safe,
To focus on my education.
The gift that I was given
Thrown away from my decision.

"What do you want to be when you're older?"
"I want to be a pilot."
The dream that I once had
Has been crushed by all the violence.

It's so dark in this place.
I see so many unusual faces,
Bruised and exploited.
They take us to random places.

The screams of excruciating pain,
The fear of being beaten,
Treated like we're animals,
To work in these conditions.

I do believe in hope.
I don't know if I deserve it,
But maybe one day,
We will be free from this purgatory.

My message to you:
Please listen to your parents.
Just follow your dreams,
Because no one is perfect.

Be careful with who you meet,
You never know who is vulnerable.
Never be afraid to speak.
The truth can be inevitable.

County Lines Uncool

Kenzo Kanapka, 15

I was walking through the park, one night after school,
seen these olders that looked cool.
They said, "You just finished school?"
I said, "Na, football."
They said to me, "Want to make some P?"
I said, "Yh, how?"
He handed me a burner phone, said, "Take this bag to the trap house in Manny!"
I said, "Say no more."
I went to the train station, got on the train.
I heard a beeping noise. I checked, it was a Nokia 365.
The gang leader said on phone,
"If u lose the bag, ur in debt."
I said I was one stop away and I realised
They was grooming me and sending me OT.
I arrived, got a taxi to the address,
Then three men in balleys ran out of an alley,
Took the bag and stabbed me.
I was left on the floor bleeding, till a group of strangers helped me
And I went back home.
The OG said, "Where's my money, fam?"
I tried to explain, I got robbed and stabbed.
He made me work till the debt was paid.
This is my story, by Jack.
Don't think selling drugs is cool.

The Knife Angel

Amelia Houghton, 17

Walking down the isolated streets,
Being innocent and sweet,
In the darkness where I have been,
In the shadows where I am seen.

After that one night,
It really gave me a fright.
Why did they pick me?
This isn't the real me…

If I knew where that night would've led,
I would've just stayed in bed.
Getting involved with a knife,
Which could now end my life.

Pressured and scared day by day,
I go home and pray.
Forced to sell these drugs,
All I want is my mother's hugs.

Going back to school with a worried cry,
Scared of whether I might die,
Regretting the decisions that led
To causing me stress in my head.

Worried to decline selling the drugs,
Frightened of these thugs,
Scared to be struck with the knife
That could deeply ruin my life.

As he held the blade to my throat,
I looked up and made a quote,
"Please, I don't want to carry on."
And after that I was gone …

Mama

Zara Khanam, 14

Mama, I did it,
I earned lots of cash.
Each one, bit by bit.
Do you have enough to stash?

Mama, the cuts still hurt
From what they did to me
After they stole my skirt.
Do you forgive my plea?

Mama, I got kicked out of school
For missing my subjects.
You said to follow only his rules.
So, do you have enough cigarettes?

Mama, I'm lost,
Left in the crowd.
I've been thrown and tossed.
Mama, are you proud?

Dark Clouds

Unaisah Dawud, 15

At first it brings friendship, hope and security.
You feel valued, you feel like you belong,
Your world has been transformed,
And there isn't a problem you can't solve.
You have all the things you could ever want:
A new phone, new trainers, happiness.

Then it turns dark;
The lights of hope get blown out.
Suddenly, you realise what a disastrous turn your life has taken,
Heavy expectations placed upon you,
Transporting tiny packages that seem to value more than gold.

Desperation.
Trapped.
Victimisation.
Heartache.
Your moral compass smashed apart.
No beaming light of hope,
Only darkness, loneliness and abandonment.

Strange Guy

Lena Rojan, 12

A sassy, strange guy
Approached us. Why?
A black hooded top;
Why did he stop
To talk to me,
In the park, at three?

He took me to his flat
To have a secret chat.
Some strangers were smoking,
Vapes they were holding.
They gave me a packet
To put in my jacket.
He handed me a phone
And told me not to moan.

I jump on the train
To get out of the rain.
I travel to a town
To see what's going down.
I get to my stop
And it's time to make the drop.
(I know this must be wrong,
But it shouldn't take me long.)

We had a knife with us,
In case of any fuss
At the end of the street,
Where we had to meet
To pick up our money.
(This wasn't very funny.)
We hand over the drugs,
And now we look like mugs
As we wait for the cash.
They were off like a flash.

I was now scared to phone
And feeling all alone.
I was now scared to phone
And feeling all alone.
Feeling all alone.
Feeling all alone.
Feeling all alone.

Gangs will be Gone

William Hickton, 14

In the UK, children suffer from dark times
Forged by the county lines.
Gangs make drugs that can be liquid or pill.
One drug, it will slowly kill…

I have information you must hear.
Do not worry, I will make it clear.
People in gangs can persuade,
To dig you up with a bucket and spade.

On the outside they seem nice,
But on the inside, their hearts are thin as rice.
Be careful because they are armed with knives,
And they will threaten your lives.

Children are targets because they are fragile and only have a young mind.
They do not see the dangers, because they are blind.
Parents, I ask you to convince them to beware,
Because the dark ones will come anywhere.

Please heed my warning.
Otherwise, you will not feel something warming.
I say, when you go from home to out there,
The black-hearted will not look, they will stare.

If you see someone and your brain starts to rust,
Talk to your parents, a teacher, a police officer, or an adult you can trust.
They can meet you, walk or even go by car.
They will be always here, near and far.

Shattered Blades

Ruby Jones, 12

Full of fear, in the shadows of the night,
Innocent lives lost with a slash of a knife.
As another victim falls, knife crimes increase.
Many lives affected, another deceased
Behind every blade, a story untold.
Parents ashamed, friends have turned cold.
There is no reason to take away a different soul.
Please put your knives away!
End knife crime across the UK.

Trapped

Immy Dunn and Sofia Pollack, 15

It was just an average day.
My parents happened to be away.

I didn't know then what was in store,
I didn't think I'd ever break the law.

He looked like a pretty dodgy man,
Then he approached me with a plan.

He pulled out a big pile of money,
And he started to call me honey.

He gave me a burner phone.
I didn't know that would be my last call home.

It started out with a few trips to Leeds.
But somehow, I never met his needs.

I tried so many times to escape.
My life just wouldn't ever reshape.

It wasn't just an average day.
I wish my parents weren't away.

Trapped 2

Immy Dunn and Sofia Pollack, 15

County lines will get you trapped.
When you've joined, your fears are unwrapped.

Don't get tempted, it's not worth it.
You know you'll never get out of the pit.

It really plays with your peace of mind,
County lines get you intertwined.

The lifestyle is not ideal;
Your identity you'll have to conceal.

You'll get found,
Get brought to the ground.

Don't try to defend,
Your life will end.

Nothing's more lonely then county lines.
You don't wanna end up in a life of crimes.

I wish I hadn't been so naïve.
Don't trust, don't join, and don't believe.

A Last Resort

Emma Jump, 15

In a world so twisted, where shadows play,
In a world so twisted, where dreams decay,
In a world so twisted, where secrets lay,
We find ourselves lost in the fray.

In towns and cities, shadows creep,
Where dreams are sold with secrets to keep.
Young lives are caught in a tangled net
Of promises made and deep regret.

Innocence lost to a darkened trade,
Where trust is broken and debts are paid.
Families torn, hearts left to pine,
In the ruthless game of county lines.

Hope still flickers, a distant light,
Hope still flickers, in the darkest night.
For every soul, a chance to mend,
To break the chains and find the end.

Caught in the net, they struggle and fight
Entangled in threads, day turns to night.
The more they thrash, the tighter it binds,
A web of deceit, where hope unwinds.

Against the bright facade lies the truth,
Harsh and scarred, it shows the proof.
Promises of gold but at what cost?
In the end, it's innocence that's lost.

A tapestry of betrayal and pain,
Where shadows rule and trust is slain.
Yet within the darkness, a light remains,
A hope that one day freedom gains.

Part 1- "I am scared"

Ibrahim Dawud, 13

I feel scared,
I feel embarrassed,
I feel trapped,
Is this the end?

What do I do,
How do I escape,
Should I run away
Or somehow stay in this living nightmare?

Will they let me go,
Will they force me to stay,
Will I live,
Will I die?
I am scared…

Part 2 "The Long Despair"

Ibrahim Dawud, 13

I awake, yet again, in despair.
Where do I go,
How do I prepare,
Is this going to flow?

The gang have expectations,
I've got trepidations.
Is this the making,
Or is this the breaking?

Will I succeed,
Will I fail,
Will I be brave,
Will I be a slave?
All I know is …. the long despair.

Time

Summer Bartlet, 15

I don't often think about the past.
It's crazy how the time goes so fast.
No more knocking at the door,
No more alcohol on the floor.
The bag's now empty,
Pills all popped.
I'm so glad that it has all stopped.
My friend was shot,
his body left to rot.
As the ambulance pulled away,
Something changed that day.
They said one more drop to go.
I told them, 'No'.
I ran home and never told my mum what happened that night.
All you need to know is, working for the people of county lines are tight.
I don't ever think about my past.
It's crazy how the time goes so fast.
When they offer you a job, make sure to say 'no'.
Run as fast as you can, it's time to go!

It's Never Just One Time

Ffyon Burnham, 13

Once I met a man, only twenty, he took me in and took care of me.
We grew closer and our friendship bloomed.
He said, "Can you take this to school?
Give it to the man outside the gate."

I did it for him just that once.
But then it happened again.
The next thing I knew, it was a spiral.
I can't get out, but I'll be fine.

He said I'm too smart for school,
But then he asked me to go to Newcastle,
"Just a short trip, that's all it'll be.
Anyways, I'll buy you a new phone just to message me."

Once was just in the past.
I now owe him favours.
He threatens me with guns.

Once I was safe.
Now violence is the only sound.
It's a spiral.
County lines should get no time.
All it is, is crime.

My Story

Keziah Needham, 13

Free bro, bro he got locked in a cage.
If you're dissing on me, I'll slap gauge,
Ruin you and your Mumsy's day.
You're done if I see you on a lack.
Olders telling me come hold this bag.
Girl's chasing me, but I don't need her.
Scored more points than I have in FIFA.
Scoring points and I don't hit the rim.
Told bro I got razors, so give opp boys a trim.
Know I done bad, but Lord accept me for my sins.
When I was young, they used to beat on me 'cause I was leng.
Now I'm older, they walk on me like concrete.
Making money, they come try stop me.
Can't believe they're tryna see me fall.
When I needed help, where was your call?
Been done wrong, I done had enough.
But I'm black hearted, I don't feel no love.
Left his white tee with a likkle red stain.
Where were you when I felt that pain?
I see guys being bad, not caring about their life.
If I could see my auntie, I would go back in time.
The day Pops left, man, I lost my mind.
So how would you feel if your brother went jail?
People by your side saying you're gonna fail.

That Life

Steve Croshaw - Community Safety Project Manager

Kids face pressures to want "that life" now,
As false peers, words, and clips tell them how.
The pull from grooming is just so strong,
As kids wrestle identity to belong.
Kids know kids who died from a blade,
As revenge, trend, or status are all overplayed.
Clips and apps show a tainted reality,
As kids post selfies by a fatality.
Toxic traits are pushed as acceptable,
As kids' minds become more susceptible.
Violence and attitude are pushed as "good",
As kids seek exposure to more than they should.
With coerced "runners" at eight years old -
Kids minds are "rewired" by what grooming sold.
Coaxed with "spiked vapes" and "drink" to impress,
As kids are abused at a "cuckooed" address.
Bright young minds are hyped to turn dark -
Online, in streets, or down at the park.
Things are seen no child should witness -
"Turned" to show "front" or indifference.
Young eyes absorb clash after clash,
Groomed to face death over debt and "cash".
Lying in hospital, kids feel misled -
Exploiters were not what they said.
Parents are left frantic with worry and fear,
As exploitation steals the child they hold dear.
Violence and abuse lurk "out there".
Animosity in society tells kids not to care.
Kids believe they want "that life" now,
As false peers, words, and clips tell them how.

Knife Sentence

Quinton Milisé - Youth Mentor & Spoken Word Artist

Have we ever stopped to ask that boy, that carries a Knife,
What he wants to do when he's older?
If his parents are still together and who his role models are?
'Cos I guarantee you, he don't live next to a Doctor.
Instead, he's more than likely to be riding with thugs,
And they're the ones in the community prescribing the drugs and
.... Driving those cars.
And I wonder if.... as a Teenager,
He's watching how the "Olders" carry themselves and it's learned behaviour.
I wonder if, by the age of 12 he never had a father,
And why, at the age of 13, he had his first balaclava.
Was he ever scared?
Is it that Mum doesn't care or is it just that she was never there?
Maybe she's out trying to provide for the family,
And by the time she gets back, she feels tired and angry.
Are there arguments at home, is there a lack of affection?
Are the boys outside offering you protection?
From the "Youts" up the road in a different postcode...
The reason why you always go the long way home!
So the "Olders" on the block become your Bigger Brothers.
Now, it's almost as if you're related to each other
... GANG-Related!
Now, we've got a Council Estate kid filled with hatred,
Who needs to be initiated, BEFORE he's fully affiliated.
Is that environment just making him numb - does
He have a choice or is it safety in num-bers...?
'Cos they're not MEANT to be your MENTORS.
That's what we need grown MEN for,
To lead by example and to nurture ambition,
To teach discipline, to understand AND to listen.

And I apologise for generalising,
For coming across like I'm stereotyping,
But we all need to know we are marginalising
A WHOLE generation when we criminalise them.
Who really wants to end up in prison or dying?
And the Social Networks make it ALL look exciting.
The way that gangs incite violence live online
And it's followed by an advert to make sure we're still buying!
And I'm not about to blame it all on DRILL,
But THOUGHTS become WORDS and words become REAL.
So tell me there's not a vested interest in what's manifesting,
When all the kids can hear is "I splashed him" and "I CHEF'D him,"
"Dipped Him" Outside of his House and then left him.
For his MUM to find him...!
Have you been to a Funeral and heard a MOTHER crying...?
When her son's in the ground, it sounds like SHE'S dying.
...It's been like this for years - wiping those tears and...
Printing those TEES!
Saying "Put the knife down."
Blaming police!
Writing to our local MPs!
I've seen mums at knife crime rallies begging on their knees,
Like... "They've took MY SON, but make it stop please!"
And it's our responsibility, have you heard?
"It takes a village to raise a Child,"
But we're losing our community, so they're left to run wild.
And this isn't the time for answers or excuses,
But the "Youngers" NEED to know there are consequences for their offences.
Justice WILL be served if you're caught or let go.
'Cos when you take a life...
You forfeit your own!

Invisible Kid

Dean Coady – OBE, SMRC, MD Urban Pure Solutions

I'm the invisible kid, you saw me yesterday,
But you just looked right through me, and you just walked away.
I'm the invisible kid, I am tired and I'm alone.
I'm the invisible kid, I am not safe in my home.
I'm the broken child, I never seem to cry,
I feel the pain and loneliness, but my eyes are always dry.
I'm the broken child, been used and cast away,
I'm the broken child, surviving day to day.
I'm the brave young kid, trying to be strong,
Doing what I must, even though sometimes it's wrong.
I'm the brave young kid and some might say I'm wild.
I'm the brave young kid, I am just a child.
I'm not asking you for answers, for the reasons I am here.
I'm not asking you for answers, just protection from the fear
That you may never see me, and I will always be
Just another victim of invisibility.
I'm the invisible kid, the kid you never see.
I just wish you'd give me back, what's been stole from me:
My innocence, my childhood and my dignity,
And I would gladly trade with you, invisibility.
I'm not asking you for answers, for the reasons I am here.
I'm not asking you for answers, just protection from the fear
That you may never see me, and I will always be
Just another victim of invisibility.

Alone

Christina Gabbitas - Author

The sadness,
The reality of a child being exploited,
Manipulated and devastated.
A tortured soul,
the physical pain,
And all for financial gain.
The stories of grief,
stories of loss.
The perpetrator, the county lines boss.
Any child can be a target -
Any background, no exemption,
fitting the exploiter profile, beyond redemption.
Debt bondage,
A cuckooed home,
Just one more burner phone.
No sleep tonight
for the exploited younger on the streets,
Homeless, and covered in dust sheets.
Missing
From home.
ALONE.

Trapped in County Lines

Christina Gabbitas - (A synopsis of the story Trapped in County Lines) with Adam Baybutt and Millthorpe School Pupils, York

Friends caught in the grip of County Lines.
If only they had heeded the warning signs.
The friends had forgotten and moved on with their lives,
Lured once again into drugs when Uncle Tony arrives.
A Snapchat invite, a friendly word,
Uncle Tony's a legend, or so Luke has heard.
A moped, free pizza, and choice of vape,
No idea what's in them, how much of a chance will you take?
Luke takes an offer he cannot refuse,
In his innocence, he has nothing to lose.
Just one little package, nothing to worry about,
Unless Luke's mum or the police find out.
At age thirteen, in Year Nine, lost and alone,
Trapped in a world he can't disown.

He is lost, vulnerable, and cornered by crime.
Social media, friendships, now all spiral out of line.
Luke's house is taken over, used as a drug den,
Cuckooed, and in debt with Dan and Ethan.
His teachers can tell that all is not well,
But Luke feels alone, with nobody to tell.
To save his skin, he takes the train to Harrogate
And drops one more package, before it's too late.
Falling into darkness in a world of despair,
Alone and silenced, but nobody's there.
Headline news, 'Fatal stabbing at pizza takeaway with loss of life'.
For Mo, it was too late at the hands of Ethan with a knife.
Luke is just thirteen years old, only in Year Nine.
He finds himself trapped in a county line.
A regular boy, with a future so bright,
Now missing, feared gone, into the darkness of the night.

Christina was accompanied by an esteemed panel of judges, including:

Anne Rannard
Protect Lead at the National County Lines Coordination Centre (NCA)

Kerrin Wilson QPM

Jim Gamble QPM
CEO of INEQE Safeguarding Group

Fran Naughton
Detective Superintendent, Head of Major and Serious Organised Crime, North Yorkshire Police

Steve Croshaw
Community Safety Project Manager

DS Sheralyn Melton
Lancashire Police

Lorraine Jones Burrell
Pastor and CEO of the Dwayne Simpson Foundation

Nathan Paul Southern
Investigative Reporter and Security Analyst

PC Mike Caulfield
Humberside Police

Dean Coady OBE
Gang and Crime Specialist, Manchester

DCI Ian Hughes
Detective Chief Inspector, Serious Violence Unit, Essex Police

Jenny Griffiths
West Yorkshire Police

Will Davis
Musician and Graphic Designer

Alicia Abbott
Animator and Character Artist

Alfie Bradley
Artist and Creator of the Knife Angel

PCSO Nick Ellis and PCSO Lisa Howie
Humberside Police

North Yorkshire Police Schools Liaison Team

Quinton Milise
Author and Spoken Word Artist

Nathan Parker
Youth Worker and Spoken Word Artist

Byron Highton
Anti Knife Crime Campaigner

Laura Bainbridge
Associate Professor in Criminal Justice, University of Leeds

Steve Arnott
Founder of Beats Bus

Adam and Brendan Storch
INIT Creative

Ann Marie Christian
International Safeguarding Consultant

Superintendent Helen Brear
West Yorkshire Police

PC Jayden Foster
Cleveland Police

Lou Hardy
Penguin Acting

Androulla Nicalaou
Child Exploitation Prevention Officer from Avon and Somerset Police

Cate Moore
Restorative Justice Independent Chair for the Lincolnshire Police Ethics
Panel

The Rabbit Hole Bookshop
Lincolnshire

David Niven
Member of the International Advisory Board at the Global Institute of Social Work

Sue McTague
Education Specialist South West

Ivan Humble
Anti Hate Campaigner

DI Suzanne Gall
County Lines Co-ordinator for West Yorkshire Police

Mandy Chapman
Retired Met Police Dog Handler

British Association of Women in Policing

Donavan Christopher
Rapper and Spoken Word Artist

Mickey Bradley
Musician with The Undertones.

Together, they contribute to a powerful movement aimed at raising awareness and addressing county lines exploitation and associated crime.

Publisher: Poems and Pictures Publishing
ISBN: 9781738507290

These stories in print and animation are designed to educate young people, providing them with the knowledge and tools to navigate these difficult issues. Christina's work plays a vital role in raising awareness and encouraging conversations around these crucial subjects.

No More Knives or 'County Lines'
Christina GABBITAS
Illustrated by Evie HURST

Link to animation.
www.nomoreknifecrime.co.uk
Commissioned by Humberside Police and Crime Commissioner

Both publications are available to buy in the NSPCC online shop.

Link to animation.
www.trappedincountylines
Commissioned by North Yorkshire Police, Fire and Crime Commissioner